Joy In The Morn'

Alayna T. Cann

Alayna T. Cann

Poetry that gives Glory, Honor, and Praise to our Lord and Savior, Jesus Christ, while uplifting the weary soul...

Psalm 30:5 ...weeping may endure for a night, but joy cometh in the morning...

Published by:

Poetry of Today Publishing
2073 Stanford Village Drive
Antioch, Tennessee 37013-4450
www.poetryoftoday.com

Book Cover Design by:
Cathi Stevenson

Library of Congress Catalog Number: 2004107179

International Standard Book Number: 0-9713885-9-8

SAN: 254-5551

Printed in the United States of America

Dedication

This book is dedicated with great reverence and honor, to my one and only, Lord and Savior, Jesus Christ. Without the Lord, and His true inspiration, I would never have been able to write, *Joy In the Morn'*. From the very title, down to the last poem, the Lord truly led me, in every aspect, of completing the book. I just want to thank and praise Him, because without the Lord, I wouldn't have been able to do it. I give God all the Glory, Honor and Praise!

I also dedicate this book to my Pastors, Dr. James and Janice Cann. You are the best Pastors anyone could ever ask for. I thank you for the many, many prayers, and support you gave me, as I endeavored to write my book. I love and appreciate you both very much!

In addition, I dedicate this book to my loving husband, Jonathan Cann. You have stood by me for many years, watching me write these poems, knowing that this was a heart's desire of mine, from the time we first met. You have always been there for me, and you have assisted me countless times. I love you always, thank you! I give special recognition to my beautiful children, Donavan, Alexander, and Christian, who were always so loving and patient with me while I spent countless hours preparing my manuscript! Thank you for your love and patience. I also thank my parents for always encouraging me to write. Thank you for your love and prayers on this journey! I love you all!

Personal Dedications

"To Touch The Hem Of His Garment"
- Dedicated to my mother Cheryl Flocken

"Just Say Yes To God"
- Dedicated to Dr. James Cann, Pastor

"Pastor, Prophetess, Mother, Friend of Mine
- Dedicated to Dr. Janice Cann, Pastor

"Heaven's Call"
- In loving, precious memory of William "Buck" Jednak 8-1-02, Family Friend

"Teach Me"
- Dedicated to Joanna Hagan, Principal Tabernacle of Praise Christian Academy

"My Guiding Light"
- Dedicated to my Husband, Jonathan Cann

"Go Ye And Witness"
- Dedicated to my Pastors, Drs. James and Janice Cann

Alayna T. Cann

4

Introduction

  Joy In the Morn' is a collection of poems that give Glory, Honor, and Praise, to our Lord, and Savior, Jesus Christ, while uplifting the weary soul. The title, comes from Psalm 30:5, "weeping may endure for a night, but joy cometh in the morning." The title tells the reader, that everyday, is a new day in Christ, it is a new beginning, and that you too, can have joy, everyday in Him! It is my prayer that this book may touch many hearts, and lives, ministering to those who need to be reminded that, "yes, weeping may endure for the night, but joy my friend, will come in the morn'!"

About the Author

Alayna Cann was born and raised in Fort Lauderdale, FL. She met her husband, Jonathan, while attending college at, Armstrong Atlantic State University, in Savannah, GA. Two years later, Mrs. Cann and her husband, were married shortly before he left, to serve in the Persian Gulf War, as a United States Marine. She and her husband now have three, beautiful, young boys.

Mrs. Cann has always had a great love for God, since a very young child, and asked Jesus Christ, to be Lord of all, in her heart and life, when she met her husband, at the age of 19 years old. She has been on fire for God, and serving Him ever since! Mrs. Cann is very proud to be a member of the "Lighthouse Tabernacle of Praise Church", in Midway, GA, where her husband's parents Pastor.

Mrs. Cann has been writing poetry since childhood, and has won numerous writing, and poetry awards throughout the years. She also was awarded a journalism scholarship in high school. She developed a real passion and love for Christian poetry during her teen years, and loves to spread the Word of God in her poetry!

TABLE OF CONTENTS

Happy Birthday My Child

"Happy Birthday my child",
I heard one happy and glorious morn',
While I knelt at an old altar,
I gave Jesus my heart and was reborn.

He forgave me for all of my sins and failures,
Wrapping His ever-loving arms around me,
Wiping away all of my tears,
In loving embrace, He enveloped my whole
being.

"Happy Birthday my child,
I have loved you forever,
I died for you,
For this I know, you shall remember."

"Share of my life and love with everyone,
Let your light so shine unto them,
Show all that it is finished, and it is done,
For great will your reward be in heaven."

"Happy birthday my child, I love you..."

John 3:3
In reply Jesus declared, "I tell you the truth, no one can
see the kingdom of God unless he is born again."

Just Say, "Yes To God!"

Living day to day,
I see the pain and tragedies of this world.

So much sadness,
So much grief,
So much anger,
So much anxiety...

If only people would open their eyes to see,
The true Living God.
If only people would open their ears to hear,
The Heavenly Father's call!

Each of us was chosen,
Each of us was bought with a price,
Each of us has a call.

The question is not,
"Where is God",
But, "Where are you?"
Are you ready?
Are you willing?

Would you sacrifice your life for Him?
Like He did for you?
Why not just take the stand and say,
"Here am I, God!"

Just Say, "Yes To God!"
(Cont'd)

Isn't it time to just lay your burdens down?
Just give them all to Him.
Isn't it time to stop living the fantasy
Of what was, nor will ever be?
Isn't it time to start living the reality
Of a true "Christ-like" life?

It's not worth it, to lose your soul to man,
But keep your soul in God.
"Man will charge you millions,
But God doesn't charge a dime!"
Why not make this your day,
And say, "yes to God?"

Psalm 4:1
Answer me when I call to you, O my righteous God. Give
me relief from my distress; be merciful to me and here my
prayer.

Pastor, Prophetess, Mother, And Friend Of Mine

Pastor of mine,
Until the end of time...

Prophetess so true,
Never say adieu...

Mother I love,
With love from above,

Teacher be near,
With great courage, and no fear...

Friend so strong,
In my heart you belong...

Pastor of mine,
Until the end of time...

Proverbs 31:28
Her children arise and call her blessed; her husband also,
and he praises her:

One Ransom

One Ransom was paid,
At Calvary's cross,
One Ransom was made,
At such great cost...

One Ransom was covered,
By the Blood of the Lamb,
One Ransom was given,
By the Great I Am....

One Ransom was paid,
So undeserved,
Making way salvation,
One Ransom was reserved...

Matthew 20:28
"..just as the Son of man did not come to be served, and to
give his life a ransom for many."

I Am Adopted

I am adopted,
By the King,
Forever in my heart,
Do glory and praises ring!

I am adopted,
By the Lord,
Forever in my heart,
He shall be adored.

I am adopted,
By my God,
Forever in my heart,
I do applaud!

I am adopted,
By my Heavenly Father,
Forever in my heart,
He shall be loved like no other.

I am adopted,
By the Master,
Forever in my heart,
I do longingly seek His face,
Desiring for Heaven to come,
Just a little faster!

Ephesians 1:5
...He predestined us to be adopted as his sons through
Jesus Christ, in accordance with his pleasure and will—

Written In Red

The words of my Savior,
Are written in red,
Bearing forth great witness,
To save the lost,
From Eternal,
Death.

Spoken in true admonition,
To encourage the weary soul,
Spoken in gentle edification,
To encourage,
The faithful.

Written in red,
His words are all true,
Spoken with immense love,
His words were written,
Just for you.

Matthew 18:14
In the same way your Father in heaven is not willing that
any of these little ones should be lost.

16

Heaven's Call

My joy escapes,
My soul expounds,
Ready for Heaven's call,
Lord, when will You beckon?

I tend to get so weary,
The test of time can cause me to fall,
Just one more day,
Lord, will I stay,
To do Your work, 'til Heaven's call.

When my time does come due,
My soul is ready,
It is waiting so intensely,
To dwell with You, Lord.

To feel such freedom,
To feel such joy,
It will be everlasting freedom,
It will be Eternal joy.

To stand in Your presence,
To look upon Your face,
To view the beauty of Your essence,
To feel, the real wonders of Your grace.

Heaven's call has now come,
It could not have come sooner,
My final test is done,
My final joy could be no truer!

Matthew 5:12
Rejoice and be glad, because great is your reward in
heaven...

Well Done, My Child

Well done, my child,
Thy race is won,
Well done, my child,
All is done.

Well done, my child,
Come join me,
Well done, my child,
Come and see.

Well done, my child,
Take thy rest,
Well done, my child,
For you, I have saved my best.

Well done, my child,
Thou has been faithful in the small,
Well done, my child,
'Tis now time to dwell with me, in the Eternal.

"Well done, my child"...

Matthew 25:23
His master replied, "Well done, good and faithful servant!
You have been faithful with a few things; I will put you in
charge of many things. Come and share your master's
happiness!

The Glory Of Heaven

The Glory of Heaven,
In all of its fullness, I do seek,
Such beauty to dwell in,
For all of Eternity, it shall please.

Just a little while more,
My Lord has said to wait,
At His appointed time, He shall open the door,
Until then, I must remain outside Heaven's
gate.

Weary not in well doing,
My Lord did say,
Hold on tight to the promise, He did tell,
"For tomorrow shall come with joy, a new day."

For the Glory of Heaven, is not so far off you
see,
You may see it in the twinkling of an eye,
Now is the appointed time, to heed the Master's
plea,
For the redeemed shall live, and never die.

Romans 2:7
To those who by persistence in doing good seek glory,
honor and immortality, he will give eternal life.

Echoes From My Heart...

There is a stirring in my heart,
It is the echoes of Your voice, Lord,
Leading me into me into Your paths of
righteousness...

There is a calling that I can hear, Lord,
It is You that I hear, the echoes of Your voice,
Resounding your Spirit's call....

There is a wooing that I feel, Lord,
It is the echoes within my heart,
Drawing me into Your great refuge and
fortress...

There is a beckoning that I hear, Lord,
It is You echoing within my heart,
Inviting me home...

I hear Your echoes, Lord,
I am now ready to heed Your Spirit's call,
The echoes beckoning from within my heart,
It's Your whisper, leading me to my Eternal
home...

Psalms 23:2-3
He makes me lie down in green pastures, he leads me
beside quiet waters, he restores my soul. He guides me in
paths of righteousness for his name's sake.

Silence Is Evidence

Silence is a witness,
To much turmoil in sight,
Evidence of God's love,
Bearing forth such steadfast Light.

Silence is His true justice,
Evidence of the tamed tongue,
Silence is never bickering,
Evidence that brings forth,
Peaceful song.

Silence is edification,
Evidence of His reward,
Silence is His witness,
Evidence of His Glory implored.
My silence is evidence of God's love...

Ecclesiastes 3:7
A time to rend, and a time to sow; a time to keep silence,
and a time to speak...

Pieces Of My Heart

The pieces of my heart,

Lord, You have so carefully defined,

Molded in Your image,

Lord, with Your love you have so diligently
refined,

Pieced together like a puzzle,

Lord, You have so creatively designed,

The pieces of my heart...

Ephesians 3:17
That Christ may dwell in your hearts by faith; that ye,
being rooted and grounded in love...

A Fire Of Love And War

I close my eyes to see you,
You are looking right back at me,
In your eyes I see a fire,
A fire of Love,
And War.

You love me,
But you also love your country,
This is why we must be apart,
It is not always so easy,
Though from God,
I have a peace that passes all understanding,
Down in my heart for you.

When I awake each day,
I think of you,
And say a prayer,
In hope, that you may return this day.

Then, when it is time to lay my head to rest,
I once again say a prayer,
This time, that there may be a new tomorrow,
Which we may one day, share together.

You are my sunshine,
And the star's dear one,
For you keep me warm,
Deep within my heart,
Therefore I will always have you to reach for.

A Fire of Love And War
(Cont'd)

And that sea that you are living next to,
Well this may be why my eyes are blue,
Because if you look real close,
I can see you.

Psalm 91:1-16

He who dwells in the shelter of the most High will rest in the shadow of the Almighty. 2 I will say of the Lord, "He is my refuge and my fortress, my God, in whom I trust."3 Surely he will save you from the fowler's snare and from the deadly pestilence. 4 He will cover you with his feathers, and under his wings you will find refuge; his faithfulness will be your shield and rampart. 5 You will not fear the terror of night, nor the arrow that flies by day, 6 nor the pestilence that stalks in the darkness, nor the plague that destroys at midday. 7 A thousand may fall at your side, ten thousand at your right hand, but it will not come near you. 8 You will only observe with your eyes and see the punishment of the wicked. 9 If you make the Most High your dwelling place— even the Lord, who is my refuge— 10 then no harm will befall you, no disaster will come near your tent. 11 For he will command his angels concerning you to guard you in all your ways; 12 they will lift you up in their hands, so that you will not strike your foot against stone. 13 You will tread upon the lion and the cobra; you will trample the great lion and the serpent. 14 "Because he loves me, "says the Lord, "I will rescue him; I will protect him, for he acknowledges my name. 15 He will call upon me, and I will answer him; I will be with him in trouble, I will deliver him and honor him. 16 With long life will I satisfy him and show him my salvation."

You Are My Vision

You are my Vision,
My soul is full of Your Spirit's call,
I am filled with a new passion,
My heart's desire is to heed Your Spirit's call,
With this I am following Your Footsteps,
You are my Vision...

To be a witness,
To just one man,
To tell of Your Excellence,
To just one more land,
You are my Vision...

In comforting one more weary soul,
You give true completion,
That makes one whole,
Bringing out Your true perfection,
You are my Vision...

Habakkuk 2:3
For the revelation await an appointed time; it speaks of
the end and will not prove false. Though it linger, wait for
it; it will certainly come and will not delay.

25

Two Hearts Beating As One

Two hearts beating as one,
We share the same Heavenly Father up above.

Two hearts in one accord,
You are my Jesus, my Savior, and Lord.

Two hearts dwelling in unity,
You died, to make me free.

Two hearts in loving embrace,
Forever on earth, I shall seek Your face.

Two hearts, perfectly one,
At Calvary's cross, all was finished, and all was
done.

Two hearts beating as one,
We are now, Eternally united as one.

We are forever,
Two hearts beating as one...

Ephesians 3:16-17
I pray that out of his glorious riches he may strengthen
you with power through his Spirit in your inner being, so
that Christ may dwell in your hearts through faith.

Do You Know How Much I Love You?

Do you know how much I love you?
Do you care for me to tell you?
Will you give me your attention?
Will you take time to fast and pray?
Just lend me your ear for the moment,
Just say yes, and wait.
You will never be disappointed,
You will never see me as late.
I will give you comfort when you need it,
I will give you joy to proceed it.
"Here am I Lord",
I would love to hear you say,
"Here am I God",
I would take pleasure in, all of the day.
Heed my supplication,
Heed my inquisition,
Listen with great patience,
Listen with great wisdom.
Diligently seek my face,
Diligently seek my vision, with decree.
My Gift to you,
An Eternal Wonder,
My Reward to you,
To be so, free.
"Now, do you know how much I love you?"

Ephesians 5:2 ...live a life of love, just as Christ loved us and gave himself up for us as a fragrant offering and sacrifice to God.

My Heart's Imperfections

Like a broken puzzle,
Were my heart's imperfections,
All jagged and worn,
They were,
From the times,
I had tried to make their connections...

I just could not comprehend,
Why their ends would not meet,
Until the day,
My heart's imperfections,
My Lord did greet...

As He smoothed away,
All of the rough edges,
Each piece fit back together, quite perfectly,
Now my heart's imperfections,
Have been mended by Him,
Making me whole, completely...

Psalm 51:10
Create in me a clean heart, O God, and renew a right
spirit within me.

Treasure Of My Heart

Treasure of my heart,
Come dwell within me,
For I, You have never forgot,
Come dwell within me freely.

Treasure of my heart,
Thou hast never failed,
Abiding always from the start,
With great victory, Thou hast hailed.

Treasure of my heart,
Thy love is so divine,
Dwell within all of my heart,
Enveloping me completely,
Throughout the end of time...

Matthew 6:21
For where your treasure is, there will your heart be also.

Vows Of The Heart

This vow I hold,
So deep within my heart,
This vow to You, Lord have I told,
Envelops the table of my heart.

This vow I hold,
Is likened to a beautiful rose that unfolds,
Resurrecting such true inner beauty,
Revealing the sanctity of my heart,
This vow Lord, for You, I do hold.

Psalms 56:12
I am under vows to you, O God; I will present my thank
offerings to you.

Ordered Of The Lord

My feet shall trod upon His paths,
My feet are ordered of the Lord.

My hands shall be lifted to Him adored,
My hands are ordered of the Lord.

My lips shall speak of His righteousness,
My lips are ordered of the Lord.

My feet shall trod,
My hands shall adore,
My lips shall implore,
My whole being is ordered of the Lord.

Psalm 37:23
If a Lord delights in a man's way, he makes his steps firm...

Welcome Home

As I drifted into slumber,
My mind did begin to unfold,
I stood in awe of Your presence,
My eyes beheld Heaven's beauty so untold,
Your gates opened wide, in all of their pearled
essence,
Every street was paved in the purest of gold.

Your arms outstretched and opened wide,
This was my final invitation to my Eternal
home.
I so hated to leave my loved ones,
But I was also ready to hear those glorious
words,
Well done my child, your race is won,
Well done, my child, welcome home!

Matthew 5:12
Rejoice and be glad, because great is your reward in
heaven, for in the same way they persecuted the prophets
who were before you.

For Love Dear One

For love dear one,
My Father gave His only Son.

For love dear child,
He shall return in a little while.

For love dear son,
We are united as one.

For love dear daughter,
He is thy Heavenly Father.

For love dear one,
All was said, all was done.

For love dear child,
On the cross, He bled and died.

"For love dear one"...

Jude 1:21
Keep yourselves in God's love as you wait for the mercy of
our Lord Jesus Christ to bring you to eternal life.

My Father's Eyes

Eyes of beauty,
Eyes to behold,
Eyes of deity,
Eyes of the untold...

Blue as Heaven,
Blue as the sea,
Blue that was given,
Blue to Thee...

Eyes so honest and true,
Eyes so faithful and flawless,
Eyes envisioned by few,
Eyes perfect even in darkness...

They are,
The Eyes of my Father,
Eyes of my God,
The eyes of my Jesus,
Eyes of His Son...

Now, won't you embrace my Father's eyes?

Psalm 34:15
The eyes of the Lord are on the righteous and his ears are
attentive to their cry...

Holy Anointing

Holy Anointing in the midst of thee,
Like the smell of a beautiful rose,
A fragrance saturating so sweetly,
His Holy Anointing magnificently overflows.

Holy Anointing rain down upon me,
Pouring out Your mercy and grace,
Holy Anointing setting me free,
Pouring out Your love in embrace.

Holy Anointing, Oh how I do love thee,
This Holy Anointing so true,
Holy Anointing, never leave nor forsake me,
I give Glory, Honor, and Praise, to You.

Song of Solomon 2:1
I am the rose of Sharon, a lily of the valleys.

Testify

Testify of the Lord,
Testify of His name adored.

Testify of God's love,
Testify of His greatness above.

Testify while here on earth,
Testify of His Son's great worth.

Testify with abundant gladness,
Testify leaving behind all sadness.

Testify to one,
Testify it is done.

Testify to all,
Testify of your call.

Testify, testify, always, testify!

I John 4:14
And we have seen and testify that the Father has sent his
Son to be the Saviour of the world.

36

Joyful Beginnings

Joyful beginnings start each day,
They are yours to have,
So arise in His praise.

Joyful beginnings are yours so free,
A life full of joy,
So wipe your eyes, then you shall see.

Joyful beginnings, His gift to you,
His Son, that was given,
In Him, we never have to part and say adieu.

Will you accept His joyful beginnings?

John 3:16
For God so loved the world, that He gave His only
begotten Son, That whosoever believeth in Him should not
perish, but have everlasting life.

A New Day

A new day has dawn,
His glory in the Son has arose,
To His glorious light I am drawn,
The saturation of His Love overflows...

My tears have all dried up,
My pain is all, but no more,
His joy has so abundantly filled my cup,
His Anointing, this day, I adore...

A new day...
He has made,
A new day,
I have bade...

A new and glorious dawn,
To this I am joyously drawn,
A new day...

Psalms 47:6
Sing praises to God, sing praises; sing praises to our King,
sing praises.

Breath Of Heaven

A Breath of Heaven,
Sent from the Father above,
A gift that was given,
For all to Love...

Bestowed upon the world to heal,
All sickness and strife,
Amended in our hearts to feel,
His Everlasting, Eternal life...

To give us just a glimpse,
Of His sacrifice for thee,
To give us just a glimpse,
Of our life thereafter to be...

A Breath of Heaven,
Dispersed upon the wings of a dove,
Such sacrifice that was given,
Through His Father's most undying, Eternal
Love...

1 John 17:3
... and this is life eternal, that they might know thee, the
only true God, and Jesus Christ, whom thou hast sent.

Whispers From Heaven

In the stillness of my heart,
I can hear whispers from Heaven,
I don't have to reach far,
All of my needs have been given.

Like a beautiful ocean breeze,
Whispers from Heaven do blow,
In your heart just believe,
His Love and Anointing shall overflow.

In even the stillness of the night,
I can hear whispers from Heaven,
Stronger than all power and might,
Voices an audible whisper from Heaven.

Heed your whisper's call,
Listen as it beckons,
From Heaven's height it does fall,
Into your heart,
It shall reckon.

Whispers from Heaven, come dwell within me,
Disperse Your Breath from Heaven,
Enveloping my whole being,
Ever so gently,
And sweetly...

Revelation 3:20
Here I am! I stand at the door and knock. If anyone hears my voice
and opens the door, I will come in and eat with him, and he with
me.

Teach Me

Teach me of Your love,
Teach me of Your peace,
Teach me of Your joy,
Teach me of Your faith...

Teach me to have Your love,
Teach me to have Your peace,
Teach me to have Your joy,
Teach me to have Your faith...

Teach me to show Your love,
Teach me to show Your peace,
Teach me to show Your joy,
Teach me to show Your faith...

Teach me Lord,
Love, peace, joy, and faith,
Teach me Lord,
Teach me...

Psalm 25:4-5
Show me your ways, O Lord, teach me your paths; guide
me in your truth and teach me, for you are God my savior,
and my hope is in you all day long.

So Free

Living with righteousness,
Living so free...

Giving unselfishly,
Giving so free...

Loving with patience,
Loving so free...

Helping kindly,
Helping so free...

Laughing with joy,
Laughing so free...

Thanking sincerely,
Thanking so free...

Forgiving honestly,
Forgiving so free...

Well done my child,
Take thy rest,
Well done my child,
Be so free...

Psalm 51:12
Restore me to the joy of your salvation and grant me a
willing spirit, to sustain me.

Beauty At Death

There is beauty at death,
In the unseen Eternal Light,
Well done, take thy rest,
Spread thy wings take flight...

Fear not my little child,
Thy race has been won,
You have trod thy last mile,
Thy reward has just begun...

There is beauty at death,
Come and dwell with me,
I invite you to take thy rest,
In absence from thy body,
Thy soul shall be free...

The most unseen beauty shall be at death.

2 Corinthians 5:8
We are confident, I say, and would prefer to be away from
the body and at home with the Lord.

By His Grace

As a child so small,
As a child so frail,
The tears did shed,
The tears did dissolve...

The Light of my God,
The Light of His Son,
Healed such pain,
Healed such hurt...

He has poured out such Love,
He has poured out such an Anointing,
Filling me with His great Love,
Filling me with His great Anointing...

My cup is now full,
My cup overflows,
Like a river of Life,
Like a river so Eternal...

By His grace,
He has saved me,
By His grace,
I am now whole.

Romans 5:1-2
Therefore, since we have been justified through faith, we have peace with God through our Lord Jesus Christ, through whom we have gained access by faith into this grace in which we now stand.

Welcome To Heaven

Welcome to Heaven,
Enter on in,
Live here forever,
Thy life shall never end,
My grace is sufficient,
Come join me my friend...

There will be no more fears,
And I will wash away all thy tears,
All thy sadness shall never be,
Come with gladness,
Give me glory...

Welcome to Heaven,
Take my hand,
Thy joy shall be again,
All souls shall triumphantly stand...

So my friend,
Welcome to Heaven,
Enter on in!

Matthew 25:21
His master replied, "Well done, good and faithful servant!
You have been faithful with a few things; I will put you in
charge of many things. Come and share your master's
happiness!"

Bask In God's Glory

Basking in God's glory,
I shall tell the world His story.

Some shall come,
Some shall go,
Never ceasing,
His Love does overflow.

As a tree planted by the water,
You shall grow,
As His son or daughter.

His Light shall shine,
Bringing forth much fruit,
As you grow,
There shall be much root.

If you plant your root in His ground,
You shall never be lost,
But always found.

As your root stretches out,
With God's love,
Reach out to others,
Stop at no boundary,
Love without doubt.

So now, just go bask in God's glory,
Always, tell the world His story.

Psalm 1:3
He is like a tree planted by streams of water, which yields
its fruit in season and whose leaf does not wither.
Whatever he does prospers.

Joy In The Morning

My heart breaks,
My soul aches,
From all, that is within me.

Oh, how I wish that I could see,
Who I really am,
Oh, how I wish that I could be,
For You, Lord, a precious gem.

From my heart I do cry,
For my desire is only to be pleasing,
My love for You,
I can't deny,
My prayers to You are never ceasing.

Please give me one more chance,
Please give me a new beginning,
For with joy I shall dance,
For my joy, shall come in the morning.

Psalm 30:5
For his anger lasts only a moment, but his favor lasts a
lifetime; weeping may remain for a night, but rejoicing
comes in the morning.

My Destiny

You have always been my Destiny,
Before my birth,
To the present,
It is so, for all to see,
In me, Your light's essence.

Your light in me is aglow,
Shining so bright it will be,
All who see, will know,
You died and set me free.

When others look at me,
I don't want to be seen,
But want Your light to shine so bright,
That they see You,
My Destiny.

A Destiny is forever,
It is Eternity,
With You, I shall dwell forever,
All who have seen shall believe!

Matthew 5:14
You are the light of the world. A city on a hill cannot be
hidden.

To Forgive

To forgive is to love,
To love is to forgive.

To forgive is to endure,
To endure is patience.

To forgive is not to judge,
To forgive is to overcome.

To forgive is to be positive,
To forgive is overlooking the negative.

To forgive is to have compassion,
To forgive is to have an open heart.

To forgive is not selfish,
To forgive is to be giving.

To forgive is to be kind,
To forgive is not to begrudge.

To forgive is to love,
To love is life everlasting.

You have been forgiven my little one...

Mark 11:24-26
Therefore I tell you, whatever you ask for in prayer,
believe that you have received it, and it will be yours. And
when you stand praying, if you hold anything against
anyone, forgive him, so that your Father in heaven may
forgive you your sins.

My Guardian Angel

My guardian angel,
Ever so gentle and true,
Sent by my Savior Jesus,
Abiding always,
Never saying adieu...

Wrapping your wings around me,
Dispersing your breath from Heaven,
Enveloping my ever-being so sweetly,
By Jesus' grace,
Your presence has been given...

Standing between me and the enemy,
Taking up thy shield and sword,
Your protection is always with me,
Surely, thou art my guardian angel,
From the Lord!

Psalm 91:11
For he will command his angels concerning you to guard
you in all your ways;

Choose You This Day

Choose you this day,
Whom you will serve...
Do you live your life?
According to His word?

Choose you this day,
How you will live...
Do you have an open heart?
Do you know how to forgive?

Choose you this day,
Where you will go...
Do you plan your footsteps?
Are they ordered of the Lord?

Choose you this day,
What you will say...
Does your tongue speak life?
Does your tongue speak death in disarray?

Choose you this day,
What you will hear...
Do you listen to the voice of God?
Do you listen to the voice of fear?

Choose you this day,
Who you will be...
Are you His chosen child?
Won't you be so free?

Choose You This Day
(Cont'd)

Choose you this day,
Your life you live, is a choice...
Will you serve Him and pray?
Will you have an ear to His voice?
Choose you this day.

Joshua 24:14-15
"Now fear the Lord and serve him with all faithfulness.
Throw away the gods your forefathers worshiped beyond
the River and in Egypt, and serve the Lord. But if serving
the Lord seems undesirable to you, then choose for
yourselves this day whom you will serve, whether the
gods your forefathers served beyond the River, or the gods
of the Amorites, in whose land you are living. But as for
me and my household, we will serve the Lord."

Jesus Loves You

Jesus loves you the same as yesterday,

Jesus loves you still today,

Jesus will love you the same tomorrow,

Jesus will love you forever and always.

Hebrews 13:8
Jesus Christ is the same yesterday and today and forever.

Let Your Words Be Few

Let your words be few,
Let your heart's meditations be refreshed anew.

Let your tongue be of silence,
Let there be no utterance of impetuous words.

Let your heart be of purity before God,
Let His presence be to you of divinity.

Let the declarations of your words to be few,
Let your dreams to be of many.

Let not your words to multiply foolishly,
Let your words to be of silence,
Let your words to be few.

Ecclesiastes 5:2
Do not be quick with your mouth, do not be hasty in your
heart to utter anything before God. God is in heaven and
you are on earth, so let your words be few.

His Word Is For You

His word is wise,
His word is true,
His word is a prize,
His word is for you...

His word is love,
His word is unselfish,
His word is complete,
His word is for you...

Psalm 119:105
Your word is a lamp to my feet and a light for my path.

Jesus, Jesus, Jesus

Jesus, my Savior,
Jesus, my Friend,
Jesus, my Master,
Jesus, my God did send...

Jesus, Eternal Wonder,
Jesus, the Great I Am,
Jesus, let no man put asunder,
Jesus, God's sign for man...

Jesus, Holy Counselor,
Jesus, Prince of Peace,
Jesus, Holy Father,
Jesus, thy Increase...

Jesus, Jesus, Jesus.

Isaiah 9:6
For to us a child is born, to us a son is given, and the
government will be on His shoulders. And He will be
called Wonderful Counselor, Mighty God, Everlasting
Father, Prince of Peace.

God's Love Divine

God's Love is Divine,
Never ceasing,
Until the end of time...

God's Love is perfect and true,
Without spot or blemish,
God's Love, will never say adieu...

God's Love is unchanging,
It is not superficial, but exchanging,
God's Love is not shallow,
But runs quite deep,
Nor is it hollow,
But stands quite steep...

God's Love is patient,
And always so kind,
With it always pleasing,
You can find...

God's Love is no secret,
You don't have to hide it,
If you openly accept it,
In your Heart, there will be no regret...

God's Love Divine
(Cont'd)

God's Love so Divine,
'Tis never temporal,
'Tis always Eternal,
Oh, so divine,
Until the end of time...

God's Love is so, Divine!

1 John 4:7
Dear friends, let us love one another, for love comes from
God. Everyone who loves has been born of God and knows
God.

Butterfly Wings And A Prayer

On butterfly wings and a prayer,
I'm going to meet Jesus in the air.

Flying skyward like a beautiful dove,
His arms outstretched, full of Love.

Welcome home my little one,
Enter on in your race is won!

1 Thessalonians 4:16-18
For the Lord himself will come down from heaven, with a loud command, with the voice of the archangel and with the trumpet call of God, and the dead in Christ will rise first. After that, we who are still alive and are left will be caught up together with them in the clouds to meet the Lord in the air. And so we will be with the Lord forever. Therefore encourage each other with these words.

My Hiding Place

You are my Hiding Place,
My shelter wherever I am,
You give me mercy and grace,
And You treat me as a precious gem.

I am covered,
By Your wings,
Oh so gentle and glorious,
Hidden by their feathers they bring,
A Heavenly Anointing,
Oh so joyous!

Because You are my Hiding Place,
There is no shelter greater,
I seek only Your face,
You are the First, the Last,
There is no other.

Yes, Lord, Yes,
You are my Hiding Place.

Psalm 91:2
I will say of the Lord, "He is my refuge and my fortress,
my God, in whom I trust."

Father Of Mine

Father of mine,
I do love so much,
Father of mine,
I do seek Your so-ever loving touch.

Father of mine,
I live for You,
Father of mine,
I shall never depart, and say adieu.

Father of mine,
I do embrace Your love,
Father of mine,
Your grace comes from above.

Father of mine,
I will dwell with You,
Father of mine,
My love for You, is all so true.

Psalm 89:26
He will call out to me, "You are my Father, my God, the
Rock my Savior."

61

The Breath Of God

The Breath of God,
From above,
Sent through His unfailing,
Enduring Love.

The Breath of God,
The Wise Men did seek,
For this they knew,
He was unique.

The Breath of God,
The angels did tell,
All who listened,
Upon their knees,
They did be-fell.

The Breath of God,
Many knew of so well,
Betrayed Him or befriended by Him,
Did they dare tell?

The Breath of God,
From Love so sweet,
Courage of strength,
With great victory,
He did greet!

The Breath Of God
(Cont'd)

The Breath of God,
Dwelling up above,
With Heaven's Breath,
Flying like a beautiful dove,
Even in death's departure,
Having filled my heart with love.

Oh, Breath of God,
Thou art Heaven's Lamb,
And the Great I Am.
Surely, Thou art the Breath of God!

1 Peter 1:18-19
For you know that it was not the perishable things such
as silver or gold that you were redeemed from the empty
way of life handed down to you from your forefathers, but
with the precious blood of Christ, a lamb without blemish
or defect.

Master

Master of my heart,
Thou dwelleth within my soul,
Master of my soul,
Thou dwelleth within my heart.

Master, the Father,
Master, the Son,
Master, the Holy Ghost,
Master, Thou art All Three In One.

Master of the universe,
Creator of all being,
Master of the human race,
Healer of all decreeing...

Master of all Heaven,
Master of all earth,
Master of all forgiven,
Master of thy birth...

Master to few,
Master to many,
Master to all,
Thou art my Master.

John 13:13
Ye call me Master and Lord: and ye say well; for so I am.

A Light In The Storm

You are a Light in the storm,
By all who see,
You shall be adored.

Great and mighty is Your Light,
A great path to all,
Both day and night...

Even through the fog it does shine,
If we open our hearts,
We can come and dine.

Lord, Your Light I shall follow,
For by faith it will lead me,
Into each new tomorrow...

Psalm 27:1
The Lord is my light and my salvation— whom shall I
fear? The Lord is the stronghold of my life— of whom
shall I be afraid?

In His Hands

My life is in Your hands,
My heart is in Your keeping,
My joy is in Your dance,
My love for You is deepening.

You are a River of Life,
From it, my heart does overflow,
You give me joy in sickness and strife,
Your love for me is a light aglow.

I am in Your Holy Hands,
You always fill my heart with joy,
With Your Liberty I shall dance,
All of the days of my life,
I will make a joyful noise.

Psalm 66:1-3
Shout with joy to God, all the earth! Sing the glory of his
name; make his praise glorious! Say to God, "How
awesome are your deeds! So great is your power that your
enemies cringe before you.

Remains Of The Day

Standing so tall and true,
Those two twin towers,
Great beacons that the world so well new...

In their final hours,
The hustle and bustle, of a New York morn'
began...
A mother arrives at work early, to make coffee
and begin her day,
A father rushes to catch a plane, for a Tuesday
morning meeting,
A daughter is heading to her office, on the 110th
floor,
And a son arrives just in time, for a conference
call, from his boss.
All has said, their daily rituals of,
"I love you, and goodbye",
To their loved ones, not knowing what their day
was to become,
Each one had intentions so well,
But only God knew their hearts...

Remains Of The Day
(Cont'd)

Whether they sensed it or not,
Their final hour was closing in,
A mighty explosion was in their midst,
Not just in the physical,
But also in the spirit of their souls...

Ascending to judgment,
Standing before the Lord,
It is either said,
"Well done, or depart from me."
Each soul then rejoices in their reward,
Or cries out in agony,
For all of Eternity,
Just in time for Eternal rest,
Or not enough time to make amends...

Who shall we remember them as today?
A faithful warrior,
Of our Savior's cross...
Or a hard, headed, rebellious individual...

There is not turning back the fate of that day,
Though it seemed like time stood still, during
that very moment...

Remains Of The Day
(Cont'd)

Don't boast about your tomorrow,
For you may not have one...
Today is your day, for that new beginning.
Don't put it off for the morrow,
For tomorrow, may never come,
Live each day, like it is your last one.

Rejoice in Him,
As He holds the future,
In His Hands...

If you died tonight,
Where might your Eternal home be?
How do you want to be remembered?

And that shall be,
The Remains of the Day....

In Remembrance of 9-11-01

1 Timothy 6:12
Fight the good fight of the faith. Take hold of the eternal life to which you were called when you made your good confession in the presence of many witnesses.

Heartbroken One

Oh heartbroken one,
Where did you go?
I so wish that I could tell you,
That I loved you more,
Than you will ever know.
Tears of sadness,
You did weep,
Tears of gladness,
Did you reap?
You lived a life of pain,
If only you knew,
You had so much more to gain.
For you God was there,
Did you know?
Did you care?
Oh, how I wanted you to know,
Of a much better place,
Where a River of Life does flow,
And oh, to see His face!
Oh, heartbroken one,
I wish that you knew,
Your life was not done,
And your days were all too few.
Will we meet again?
I shall only know in due time.
God will always be my friend,
There is no one greater,
For you to find!

Psalm 147:3
He heals the brokenhearted and binds up their wounds.

Go Ye And Witness

I am a witness
Yes I am,
I am a witness,
For By the Blood of the Lamb.

Go ye,
In all of the land,
Be a witness,
For the Great I Am.

Go witness here,
Go witness there,
Go ye,
Witness everywhere.

Go ye, to one,
Go ye, to all,
Go ye, take the call.
"Go ye and witness."

John 1:7
The same came for a witness, to bear witness of the Light,
that all men through him might believe.

True Joy

My heart is filled with joy, oh Lord,
From all that is within me,
For You, oh Lord, are the one to be adored,
There is no other that I can see.

Like the sun is to the flower,
You are the Light to me,
In the needed hour...

You gave Your life for me,
I give my all to You,
You give me life more abundantly,
My return to You, is all too few.

Each day, oh Lord,
I will give my praises to Thee,
From this time forth,
Throughout all Eternity...

Lord, You are my true joy!

I John 1:4
...that your joy may be full.

My Visions

My visions are many,
Reaching to the height of Heaven,
Envisioning all of Eternity.

I see Angels all around me,
And the magnificence, of their awesome essence,
My soul feels so free,
My desire is to dwell among their presence.

My visions are of the Throne of the Lord,
I am now standing at His side,
He is showing me all the Glory on earth, to me
He implored,
For this homecoming day, my soul He did guide.

I can see the ambience of Heaven, in all of it's
Glory,
Such breathtaking beauty to behold,
It is such true joy,
To be unfold.

As a promise from my Lord,
I see a rainbow in the clouds,
If by Grace, I am in accord,
For all of Eternity in Heaven, I shall be found.

My visions are many,
Reaching to the height of Heaven,
My visions are set on all Eternity.

2 Peter 1:4
Whereby are given unto us exceeding great and precious
promises...

Please Forgive Me

Please forgive me,
I knew not the pain, that I might cause,
Please forgive me,
I was in the world, and not living for You God...

Please forgive me,
My heart does say,
Please forgive me,
I shall unceasingly pray...

Please forgive me,
My trespasses evermore,
Please forgive me,
For many treasures, You have laid up in store...

Please forgive me,
For my life, I am giving to You,
Please forgive me,
For to this world, I have said adieu.

Please forgive me...

Romans 10:10
For with the heart man believeth unto righteousness,
with the mouth confession is made unto salvation.

The Joy Of My Heart

The joy of my heart,
The salvation of my soul,
Overflows like a river,
Bringing me peace,
Making me whole...

My cup runneth over,
With thy Anointing so full,
Saturating my whole being,
Overwhelming me completely,
Sending the enemy fleeing...

This joy You have placed in my heart,
And the salvation of my soul,
Is the awesome Anointing of the Holy Ghost,
And He dwells within me forever,
To reign and rule...

I John 1:4
And these things write we unto you, that your joy may be
full.

Tears Before Heaven

Tears before Heaven,
The heart does shed,
Such joy unleavened,
Such peace unsaid.

No tears to be shed,
For the soul up there,
Such joy unspeakable,
Such peace is there.

Tears of joy,
Tears of peace,
Tears no more,
Throughout all Eternity forever,
Him we shall adore.

Psalm 126:5
They that sow in tears shall reap in joy.

I Envision

I envision Heaven,
I envision You,
I envision all that You have given,
I envision only what is true.

I envision only, to give,
I envision Your face to see,
I envision myself in Heaven with You,
Lord to live,
I envision to be, so free, for all of Eternity,

I envision...

Psalm 19:1
The heavens declare the glory of God...

Sealed In His Kingdom

In the palm of God's hands,
My heart and soul does lie,
Of such great love and compassion He doth give,
When my heart does cry.

Healing and soothing,
His breath I do feel,
'Tis such Holy Anointing,
'Tis almost surreal...

His touch is so gentle and divine,
Soft as a dove's feather,
Completely enveloped through all of time,
I shall be sealed in His kingdom forever.

2 Timothy 4: 18
And the Lord shall deliver me from every evil work, and
will preserve me unto his heavenly kingdom: to whom be
glory for ever and ever. Amen.

Peace, Love, And Grace

Peace,
Peace be still,
Peace,
Listen to God's will.

Love,
Love from above,
Love,
Love as a gentle dove.

Grace,
Seek God's face,
Grace,
For you, he has prepared a place.

Peace, Love, and Grace,
For you, and for me,
All for the world to see,
Far,
Beyond even, Eternity....

Peace, Love, and Grace…

Proverbs 8:17
I love them that love me; and those that seek me early
shall find me.

I Am A Soul Survivor

I am a soul survivor,
For You Lord, I am on fire!

With a fire shut up in my bones,
I stand on a Solid Rock,
Not just a stone...

There is a great fire in my dance,
Thank You Lord,
For my second chance!

Chances as they are,
They can come both near and far...

Come as they may,
No matter what,
You are here for me everyday!

Because of You,
I am now a soul winner,
The numbers can be few,
Oh, if just to save one sinner!

Now I am a soul survivor, and a soul winner!

Psalm 27:5
...he shall set me upon a rock.

Friend

Friend of mine,
Until the end of time...

Friend so true,
Never say adieu...

Friend I love,
With love from above...

Friend be near,
With great courage and no fear...

Friend so strong,
In my heart you belong...

Friend of mine,
Until the end of time...

Proverbs 17:17
A friend loveth at all times...

Well Done, Well Done, Well Done

Now is the appointed time,
To stand for the Lord,
'Tis not the time,
To sow in seeds of discord...

For the fervent prayer,
Of the righteous man availeth much,
You are of His every care,
Keep seeking His ever-loving touch...

Because if you'll seek ye first,
His Kingdom,
Ye shall never hunger nor thirst,
But forever dwell with Him in freedom...

So weary not in well doing,
We should be instant in every season,
It is His perfect will to keep, in continuing,
For He knows all rhyme and reason...

Question not our Heavenly Father,
Honor His word,
For Father knows best, like no other,
He loves each of us as His own,
All of our petitions has He ever heard...

In sickness,
He will make you whole,
In meekness,
Your cup shall ever be on earth full...

Well Done, Well Done, Well Done
(Cont'd)

One day ye shall receive His embrace,
Well done my little one,
You have completed your race,
All on earth is done….

Enter on in,
To thy joy,
Enter on in,
To thy rest,
Well done, well done, well done...

James 5:16
The effectual fervent prayer of a righteous man availeth
much.

Matthew 6:33
But seek ye first the kingdom of God, and his
righteousness; and all these things shall be added unto
you.

Galatians 6:9
And let us not be weary in well doing: for in due season
we shall reap, if we faint not.

James 5:15
And the prayer of faith shall save the sick, and the Lord
shall raise him up...

Matthew 25:21
...enter thou into the joy of thy lord.

Healer Of My Heart

Oh, Healer of my heart,
All broken and battle worn,
Are my wounds and scars
Echoing from the deepest valleys of my soul,
Desiring to cleave unto Thee,
So by You,
A new creature I'll be,
Completely, made whole...

Oh, Healer of my heart,
For You, a living sacrifice,
My desire, 'tis to be,
For at Calvary's tree, You paid the price,
Prepare me, to be pure and holy...

Oh, Healer of my heart,
Without You, so destitute I am,
Perfection of your will, I surely do seek,
The stronghold of the enemy, I shall refuse...

Oh, Healer of my heart,
I feel Your gentle embrace,
Very softly and tenderly,
I do forever seek, Your Pure and Holy face,
My love for You, Lord is forever,
It is unchanging, it is unending...

You are, the Healer of My Heart...

Ezekiel 18:31
...and make you a new heart and a new spirit...

I Live

I live for Jesus,
I live for God,
I live for the Lord,
I live for Him alone, only...

I live with faith,
I live with hope,
I live with grace,
I live with love...

I live freely,
I live joyfully,
I live wholly,
I live peacefully...

I will live with Him everlastingly,
I will live with Him forever,
I will live with Him Eternally,
I will live with Him evermore...

Psalm 119:175
Let my soul live, and it shall praise thee...

Life Is A Vapor

Life is like a vapor,
For just awhile it appears,
Though seemingly lasting forever,
To dwell with Him, will be no more tears.

On earth,
So much pain and sadness is reaped,
But through His redemption, is new birth,
And forever you shall be freed,

So remember,
Life is like a vapor,
Just appearing for a season,
Give your life to Jesus, the Savior,
For who He is, is all the reason!

Never forget...Life on earth...is a vapor...

James 4:14
Whereas ye know not what shall be on the morrow. For
what is your life? It is even a vapor, that appeareth for a
little time, and then vanisheth away.

Seeds Of Morality

The seeds of morality,
Are being planted everywhere,
The sins of reality,
Are being committed without care...

All innocence is lost,
For at great prices paid,
All recompense could never humanly pay the
cost,
For such defeated sacrifices made...

A disservice that has been rendered,
Acts of desperation upon the heart and soul,
Choices that have been surrendered,
Now is a culmination of cries to be forgiven, and made
whole.

Never a deaf ear,
Does God have for a fallen man,
One should come to Him with confidence,
having no fear,
For we, are given the choice to follow His plan.

1 John 1:9
If we confess our sins, He is faithful and just to forgive us
our sins, and to cleanse us from all unrighteousness.

True Submission

As I kneel humbly at Your feet,
With Your loving touch,
Lord, do You greet...

My heart desperately in need,
You are my Shepherd, Lord,
To my soul that feeds...

As my Heavenly Father,
In loving embrace,
Holding me like no other,
Cleaving me in place...

My true submission,
Obedience to Your will,
My true passion,
Love for You, to be fulfilled...

Hence, I give You my "True Submission"...

Isaiah 1:19
If ye be willing and obedient, Ye shall eat the good of the
land...

I Have Set My Affection On Things Above

I have set my affection on things above,
I have set my sights on Heaven,
In Heaven I will dwell with the one I love,
In Heaven is much joy to be leaven...

I seek only my love's face,
I seek only my love's favor,
In welcoming to receive His embrace,
In Honor of Him, I shall never waver...

Offering praises of glorification,
To my Heavenly Father,
The tranquility of His rest, I shall receive,
Offering praises of exaltation,
To Jesus, my Savior,
The serenity of His joy, I shall achieve...

I have set all my affection on things above....

Colossians 3:2
Set your affection on things above, not on things on the
earth.

Home, Free At Last

My heart leaps and abounds,
As Heaven's trumpet now sounds,
Rejoicing to angelic hymns,
As praises to my King,
Forever ring!

Enchanted by the glow of Heaven's light,
Strolling down the streets of gold,
Enjoying the Heavenly sights...

My soul is now home at last,
Dwelling with my Lord,
To roam so free and vast,
Forever praising Him adored.

I am home, free at last...

Revelation 21:21
And the twelve gates were twelve pearls; every several
gate was of one pearl: and the street of the city was pure
gold, as it were transparent glass.

Heaven Bound

I am Heaven bound,
My heart leaps for joy,
Oh, to hear the glorious trump' sound...

On this journey as I travel,
The road isn't always smooth,
As I may stumble,
In the pits of the gravel...

So bound for Heaven I am,
No road is too crooked for me,
For I do seek "The Great I Am"...

I shall be forever, Heaven bound,
Unceasingly traveling life's journey...
For once as a sinner I was lost,
In Him, I am Eternally found...

Until the glorious day,
I reach Heaven's gate...
I'll always be Heaven bound,
For to dwell with my Lord, 'tis my fate...

So faithfully, I am Heaven bound...

Psalm 100:4
Enter into his gates with thanksgiving, and into his
courts with praise: be thankful unto him, and bless his
name.

Farewell

Farewell I say,
Farewell to all,
Farewell today,
Farewell my Savior does call...

Farewell my dear,
Farewell my friends,
Farewell no more tears,
Farewell all is done...

Farewell this day,
Farewell be near,
Farewell I pray,
Farewell is here...

Farewell does come,
Farewell 'tis true,
Farewell my loved ones,
Farewell to you...

Farewell my love,
Farewell so true,
Farewell, but for just a little while,
Farewell, I must say adieu...

Farewell...I will always Love you...

I Peter 1:8-9
Whom having not seen, ye love; in whom, though now ye
see him not, yet believing, ye rejoice with joy unspeakable
and full of glory: receiving the end of your faith, even the
salvation of your souls.

Love Letter To God

Dear God,

I Love You deeply,
I love You wisely,
I love You uniquely,
I love You contritely,
I love You meekly,
I love You more than yesterday, God...

I love You completely,
I love You only,
I love You freely,
I love You wholly,
I love You more than today, God...

I love You passionately,
I love You faithfully,
I love You infinitely,
I love You joyfully,
I love You more than tomorrow, God...

I love You divinely,
I love You continually,
I love You gloriously,
I love You purely,
I love You warmly,
I will love You forever, Eternally, God...

Love Always, Your Child...

Psalm 31:23
O love the Lord, all ye his saints...

Pains Of The Heart

Pains of the heart,
Sadness of the soul,
Joy looms off afar,
If only to be made whole...

Tears of loneliness,
Bears my sadness,
Fears of discontentedness,
Shares my weariness...

Mold me, Lord,
Refine me, Lord,
Hold me, Lord,
Abide with me, Lord...

Refreshed and anew,
Dwelling always in You,
Until my Eternal dawning,
Hide me 'til each morning...

Psalm 18:6
In my distress I called upon the Lord, and cried unto my
God: he heard my voice out of his temple, and my cry
came before him, even unto his ears.

To Touch The Hem Of His Garment

To touch the hem of His garment,
Is to be made whole,
To touch the hem of His garment,
Is to be touched, way down in my soul.

To touch the hem of His garment,
Forever changed I'll be,
To touch the hem of His garment,
Forever, I'll be so free.

To touch the hem of His garment,
Is my, fortress and protection,
To touch the hem of His garment,
Is my, divine connection!

To touch the hem of His garment,
His Salvation, I have received.
To touch the hem of His garment,
His Life-everlasting, I shall achieve.

Matthew 9:21
For she said within herself, If I may but touch His
garment, I shall be whole.

Eternal Joy

I am now in flight,
To the One and Only,
In all of His might...

As I enter into His presence,
I shall lift holy hands unto Him,
In honor of His great essence,
I will be on bended knee to Him...

My lips shall praise of His magnificence,
Tears will be shed crying, Holy, Holy, Holy,
His Angels shall sing praises as His witness,
Eternal peace will be my joy, joy, joy!

I have now entered into His final promise,
The one He so lovingly made,
That we might one day dwell in His Eternal
presence,
In His death on the cross, the foundation was
laid,
Eternal peace is my joy!

Psalms 126:5
They that sow in tears, shall reap in joy.

I Do Need Thee

Hold me,
Cleave me,
Love me,
Comfort me,
Don't leave me, Lord,
I do need thee…

Rescue me,
Save me,
Protect me,
Don't leave me, Lord,
I do need thee…

Hear me,
Answer me,
Change me,
Don't leave me, Lord,
I do need thee…

I'll praise thee,
I'll love thee,
I'll glory in thee,
I am Your child, Lord,
I'll forever need thee…

Receive my soul unto thee,
As I praise You with great expectancy,
Satisfying thee,
For Eternally, I do need thee, Lord…

Psalm 62:1
Truly my soul waiteth upon God, from him cometh my salvation.

I Give You Glory, Honor, And Praise

My heart is filled with silence,
My soul is still,
I give You, Glory, Honor, and Praise, Lord,
For Your will...

You have created within me,
A clean heart,
Mercy, You have poured out upon me,
Through Your loving, compassion...

Oh, how I praise You, Lord!
For You have rescued me,
From the loud hush,
And tormenting snares of the world...

I shall sing Psalms to You,
In thanks and praise, for my salvation.

In my heart and soul,
Dwells hunger and thirst,
For Your word, Oh Lord,
Which I shall feed upon...

In the darkness of the night,
I cry out to You,
In fear of what is known,
And what is not...

But...I will always,
Give You Glory, Honor, and Praise,
Because I live for You Lord, not for the world...

Psalm 89:5
And the heavens shall praise thy wonders, O, Lord...

My Guiding Light

In the midst of the night,
On one such as tonight,
I lift my hands toward Heaven,
And I see a light,
It is You, Lord,
You are my Guiding Light.

During nights such as these,
You remind me,
That with You as my Guiding Light, Lord,
There will be no more lonely nights.

I cherish these nights with You, Lord,
For they are the Alpha and Omega of each day
here,
Carrying this thought in my heart,
There will be no more lonely days.

For You are my Guiding Light, Lord,
You pick me up, when I may falter,
You make me to smile, if I am ever to frown,
Your light carries me into each new tomorrow,
Mending my heart, which may be filled with
sorrow.

Oh how Your light shines so bright, Lord,
Where there are raging waters,
In the loud hush of the world,
Your Light pours still ones,
In my heart,
To be restored.

My Guiding Light
(Cont'd)

Though the journey may be long,
That I have here, to do for You,
But 'tis not so long with Your Shepherding...
Light, Lord.

To man, I am just a soldier of the world,
But to me, and Your Light,
I am a soldier for the Lord.

Yes, Lord, it is true...
You will forever,
Eternally, be my Guiding Light.

Dedicated to my husband Jonathan Cann...I wrote this to him while he was serving in the Persian Gulf War, as a US Marine, with ground troops. 03/26/1991

2Timothy 2:3
Thou therefore endure hardness, as a good soldier of
Jesus Christ.

Dear Jesus

Dear Jesus,
Wake me when the sun shines,
And please overshadow me through each new
tomorrow...

Wherever there is hatred,
Please bless me with Your abundant Love,
Wherever there be pain or hurt,
Please bless me with Your abounding Joy,
Lord, Please hold my hand,
Not only in darkness, but throughout my
lifetime...

Dear Jesus,
I will always need You,
You will always be my life, inspiration, and
everything!
Through You, I have fulfilling Faith,
With this Faith, You help me to fight each
battle,
And I am able to shout "VICTORY" in the end!

Dear Jesus,
I just wanted to say that I love You and praise
You...

1 Samuel 17:47
...the battle is our Lord's...

My Tribute

My tribute to You,
Could never be enough,
All the words I'd have to say,
Would be all to few,
So with humble adoration,
I give You my praise...

In tribute,
I'll give, my heart each day,
On bended knee, for the lost,
I'll unceasingly pray,
No matter what the cost...

My tribute to You,
I just want to say,
I'll love You Lord, Forever,
Each and every day!

With this I give, "My Tribute"...

Romans 13:7
Render therefore to all their dues: Tribute to whom
tribute is due; Custom to whom custom; Fear to whom
fear; Honor to whom honor.

The Gem Of Eternity, The Crown Of Expectancy

I cry out to You,
From the depths of my heart,
Loneliness looms,
In the distance of the dark...

I lift my hands unto You,
Oh Holy most High,
Tears on Thy cheeks,
Rain down from the sky...

The essence of Your beauty,
So secretly untold,
The presence of Your deity,
So richly unfold.

Hidden by Heaven,
The Gem of Eternity,
Revealed through Salvation,
The Crown of Expectancy!

Received in the twinkling of an eye,
My joyful beginning,
Achieved, no more shall I cry,
For with You,
In Heaven I am dancing and singing!

Psalm 62:5
Find rest, O my soul, in God alone; my hope comes from him.

The Sinner's Prayer

Jesus,
I ask You to come into my heart,
Always to rule and reign;
Forgiving me, cleansing me,
Removing every stain,
Giving me a new start.

Wash me white as snow,
Making me completely whole.
Mold me, and make me,
Renew me, and refine me as pure gold.

As I repent of all my actions,
I thank You for Your great sacrifice.
Accepting Your grace, with humble satisfaction,
Knowing for me, You paid the ultimate price.

With myself, unworthy of anything,
I have asked You to be,
My Jesus, Lord, and Savior.
So that with praises I might sing,
And in Heaven, dwell with You in favor.

Romans 10:9-10
That if you confess with your mouth, "Jesus is Lord," and
believe in your heart that God raised him from the dead,
you will be saved. For it is with your heart that you
believe, and are justified, and it is with your mouth that
you confess and are saved.

NOTES

NOTES

NOTES

NOTES

NOTES

NOTES

NOTES

Poetry of Today Publishing

www.poetryoftoday.com

Spreading the Words of God Through Poetry!

Poetry of Today Publishing
2073 Stanford Village Drive
Antioch, TN 37013-4450

<u>Other Titles by Poetry of Today Publishing</u>

If you would like to order other titles published by Poetry of Today Publishing, check the book(s) desired, complete the form below and mail it with your payment to the address provided. Our books make great gifts!

_____ My Life Is Like A Story - $8.00
_____ Every Eve - $8.00
_____ Thank God for Salvation - $8.00
_____ Reflections on Life - $8.00
_____ Lord's Tears - $10.00
_____ I Love Jesus Christ - $8.00
_____ You Are Not Alone In A Lonely World - $8.00
_____ Human Race Evaluate - $10.00
_____ The Heart Cries - $8.00
_____ Joy In The Morn' - $8.00

Add $2.50 per book for shipping and handling for each book.

Name: _____
Address: _____
City/State: _____
Zip: _____

(Orders are shipped within five days of receipt.)